The Lump Sum Pension Payment Guide

Joel M. Johnson, CFP®

Printed in The United States of America

ISBN: 978-15447245515

Big Man Publishing

Contents

Chapter 6

What Are The Risks And Rewards?

Chapter 7

What Are The 6 Things Not To Do?

Chapter 8

Should I Have A Retirement Income And Financial Plan?

Conclusion

Regulatory Issues

Notes to Readers

This publication contains the opinions and ideas of its author. The strategies outlined in this book may not be suitable for every individual and are not guaranteed or warranted to produce any particular results.

Presentation of performance data herein does not imply that similar results will be achieved in the future. Any such data are provided merely for illustrative and discussion purposes; rather than focusing on the time periods used or the results derived. The reader should focus instead on the underlying principles. This book is sold with the understanding that neither publisher nor author, through this book, is engaging in rendering legal, tax, investment, insurance, financial, accounting or other professional advice or services. If the reader requires such advice or services, a competent professional should be consulted. Relevant laws vary from state to state.

No warranty is made with respect to the accuracy or the completeness of the information contained herein, and both the author and the publisher specifically disclaim any responsibility for any liability, loss, or risk, personal or otherwise, that is incurred as a consequence, directly or indirectly, of the use and application of any of the contents of this book.

The ideas expressed are not meant to be taken as advice that you can act upon.

You should find an individual advisor that you trust to implement these ideas after determining if they are appropriate and suitable for your unique situation.

Insurance Products and Annuities are guaranteed by the insurance companies themselves. The safety of these accounts is dependent on the claims paying ability of the insurance companies.

Introduction

This may be the biggest decision you've ever had to make in your life: whether to take your pension in the form of monthly payments - as it was probably promised to you when your employment began - or take it as a lump sum one-time payment and roll it over into an Individual Retirement Account (IRA).

This book was written to help you make that decision, and better understand the pros and cons of the choices you have. You are not alone. This is a decision that many people have had to make and, quite frankly, many people are intimidated by. As you read through these chapters, your understanding should increase, and your anxiety should diminish. It is an important decision to make, with ramifications that could last through your lifetime, and into the lives of future generations. So taking it seriously, evaluating your options, and acting thoughtfully can make a big difference. It could be the difference between having a very comfortable life financially but with nothing to pass on in the future (whether it would be to children or grandchildren), or taking control of your money and leaving a significant legacy. There are, however, potential consequences to consider if you elect to take investment control of that money. That is what we examine here, with the easy-to-understand guide that you now have in your hands. Johnson Brunetti is a registered investment advisor, registered with the Securities and Exchange Commission (SEC). We are also licensed insurance brokers. I am majority owner of the firm. We have been helping retirees in the Northeast for more than ten years in structuring their retirement plans. I have been in the business since June of 1989, but since 2004 we have focused solely on working with individuals (and families) that are either already retired or getting close to retirement. Because so many companies, by in effect forcing retirement, put people in a position where they must make this decision relatively quickly and often unexpectedly, I have designed this guide to provide you with the basics you'll need to help in your decision-making. Now, let's begin considering whether taking a lump sum, or taking monthly pension payments from the company, would be the better choice for you and your family.

Chapter 1

Why is my company doing this?

In this chapter, we are going to explain why corporations of virtually every size and industry all over the world, but especially in the United States, give you the option to take a lump sum payment upon retirement, instead of beginning a monthly pension payment.

But let's begin at the beginning, and briefly talk about what a pension is.

Fundamentally, your pension is a promise that the company has made to you, to provide you with money when you retire. Because the company has made you that promise, at some time in the future they are going to have to pay out money to you.

Let's illustrate that with an example: You started working at a company at age 30, and their pension plan says that if you work until age 65 the company will pay you $5,000 a month for the rest of your life.

It also says that if you take a little less than $5,000 a month, they will pay you that money for the rest of your life and your spouse's life, if you were to die first - and it is completely guaranteed by the company.

The chart may look something like this:

Pension Options			
Age	Option	Your Monthly Income	Your Survivor Gets Upon Your Death Monthly
65	Single Life	$5,000	-0-
65	50% Joint Survivor	$4,500	$2,250
65	100% Joint Survivor	$4,000	$4,000
65	Single Life with 10 Year Certain	$4,800	Survivor only gets the remainder of the 10 years of payments from the original start date

The company did not have to put any money aside to back the pension – but they have made you a promise that they will pay a certain amount at your retirement. Because they have made that promise, you become a creditor of the company by having that pension on the books of the company as a promise of future payments that they have made. Keep in mind that a public company has to show its future pension liabilities – those promises- as a debt on its balance sheet. So, the company we've used in this example must predict, for all the workers they have on the books, about how long each of them is likely to live and how much the company can earn on money the company has set aside until then. Then they do set money aside based on these calculations. The company also needs to show the results of that analysis, their future pension liabilities, as a debt on the company balance sheet. There it sits, as a very large number - future pension liabilities. The amount of money in their investment account backing the pension is, of course, an asset. Now that we understand what a pension is, from the company's standpoint, it is easier to understand why companies would offer you a lump sum instead of monthly payments, when you retire.

They would rather not have that future liability sitting there on their balance sheet. They would much rather clean it up, give you a lump sum, and be done with it. It is a big, future uncertainty that they cannot control.

It is also important to keep in mind that the obligation to pay – the company's promise to you - gets larger or smaller as it remains on the company balance sheet based on three main factors.

Discount Rate

The first factor that can make the anticipated obligation larger or smaller is the current interest rate, or as actuaries call it, the discount rate. Basically, companies have to make an assumption as to what they will be able to earn on their money until it is time to start paying you when you retire. Let's say, for example, that the company assumes they will earn three or four percent. Those projections also change over time, and a lower discount rate implies an increase in pension expense, an increase in future liability.

It can best be described as a seesaw. One side of the seesaw is the future liability, the other side of the seesaw is interest rates. When interest rates go down, the discount rate goes down, therefore the liability goes up. When interest rates go up, the liability goes down on the other side of the seesaw.

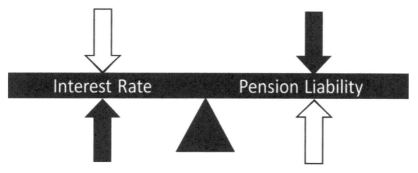

Life Expectancy

The next factor that can come into play and affect the obligation is life expectancy. People are living longer. Here's why that matters, from the company's perspective.

Let's say that 50 years ago when your company put its pension in place, the average life expectancy of its workers might have been 67 to 70 years old. Fast forward to today. The average life expectancy is reaching 80 and beyond. When the pension plan was instituted, the company anticipated a certain amount that they would have to pay out, based on life expectancy in retirement. Now people are living much longer, and because they're living longer the company will be obligated to pay out much more than they originally planned. This obviously adds uncertainty, which companies don't like, and can have a substantial impact on their potential liability.

Investment Earnings

The third factor that affects whether the company's future pension payment obligations will be larger or smaller is the potential for future investment earnings.

Companies don't know with any certainty what they are going to earn on their investments, and that can be an important variable. To illustrate that, let's consider two scenarios:

- Company A earns seven percent, over the long-term, on its investments. That additional income will go a long way towards making up for some of their future obligations. They do not have to fund their investment account as much because they're earning more on each dollar invested.

- Company B earns considerably less than that on its long-term investments. That means they may need to kick in some extra money to pay their future pension obligations. That puts more financial pressure on the company, as the liabilities loom large and investment earnings don't do as much to reduce it.

Your Choice, Their Balance Sheet

To summarize, company pension plans – their promise to pay you when you retire – are affected by three main factors: current interest or discount rates, life expectancy of workers, and the amount of money the company can earn on its investments. Each of these factors and all of them together, can have a significant impact on the massive liability that a company is carrying on its books for the future. If your employer is a publicly traded company, then they care what the analysts think, and Wall Street analysts hate uncertainty and large liabilities.

That is why your company is giving you the choice at retirement of taking a lump sum or taking monthly payments. The bottom line for the company in regards to pension payments is very uncertain – with factors in constant motion that can, and do, affect the size of the pension liability sitting on their books. They are under a lot of pressure from Wall Street to lessen that uncertainty, so they would rather clean up the uncertainty than continue to have it weigh down the balance sheet.

To get that uncertainty off the books, and reduce that unpredictable and enormous liability, they are hoping that as many people as possible elect to take the lump sum payment upon retirement.

When that happens, the company makes the lump sum payment and they can clean up that looming pension liability and get it off their books. The decisions are made one pension recipient at a time; the cumulative impact of many individuals deciding to take the lump sum can make a substantial difference in the company's pension liability.

Chapter 2

What are My Options?

As you evaluate your options, it is important to understand that depending whether you choose monthly payments or lump sum, you may be shifting the investment risk from the company to yourself.

If you take a monthly payout, that risk is on the company. They guarantee your payments, month after month, for the rest of your life. (And there is the federal government's Pension Benefit Guaranty Corporation which stands behind your company within certain limits in case they were to go bankrupt.)

On the other hand, you decide to take a lump sum payment; you have many potential benefits, but you are now responsible for investing the money (or you need to identify and retain a financial advisor to manage that investment for you). In my experience, most people choose to rollover a lump sum to an IRA but it's important to understand there are pros and cons to each choice.

As we discuss your options in this chapter, we will break them down into the two basic choices you have. But in each instance, there are also numerous sub-options – choices you can make that will affect the payment you receive. As we proceed, these will be highlighted as well.

For instance, should you decide to stick with the traditional monthly payment for the rest of your life, there are some additional choices you can make, once you've made that initial decision. You can take slightly less each month and have the payments continue throughout your spouse's life, should she live longer. You could also decide to take the monthly payments, but indicate that if you do not live for ten years, you want a guarantee that payments will continue for ten years, which could be beneficial for your family. So, there are a number of choices even after you've made the threshold decision on lump sum versus monthly payments. We will illustrate that later in this chapter. Before getting into the more intricate details, let's spend some time examining the initial critical choice that needs to be made:

taking a lump sum for your pension versus leaving things as they are and going ahead with the monthly payout.

Option One: Lump Sum Payment

If you elect to take the lump sum, you are proceeding with an IRA rollover. You are rolling the money from the pension over to an IRA, tax-free if done properly, and then you are going to invest the money so that you have the opportunity to pay out to yourself, based on your monthly needs. There are advantages and disadvantages of that approach.

As was mentioned earlier in this book, you would now be taking on the investment risk. You would be responsible for investing the money, which many people would view as a disadvantage, precisely because the risk is being shifted to you - or you along with your team of financial advisors. Others would argue it is an opportunity, depending upon their degree of confidence in your – or your teams' - investing expertise. You could do better.

Another potential disadvantage to consider is if either

you or your spouse are "not good" with money, and you tend to spend too much. If that is an appropriate description, you may not want to give yourself access to the pension money through a lump sum payout.

If you don't trust yourself, if you are a person with a track record of running up credit card debt or spending excessively, living beyond your means, it may make more sense for you _not_ to take the lump sum. It is a matter of being better safe than sorry – the dependable monthly payment may be a better choice than having your entire pension benefit paid all at once just as you start retirement, leaving you with the temptation to squander it as you may have done with other money in the past. Most of our clients do not fall into that category. They tend to be very good with money and are good savers.

But there are some individuals who should not take the lump sum for those reasons. As with many of life's decisions, you need to know yourself.

To summarize, the primary reasons not to elect the lump sum are:

- It is a challenge for you to control your spending.
- You would be shifting some of the investment risk away from the company and to you.

Now let's move on to outline the positive aspects of the lump sum option. Advantage number one is <u>control</u> - you can control your payments. Advantage number two is <u>flexibility</u>.

I would estimate that out of every ten people that we work with in our office who have an opportunity to take a lump sum pension payment, nearly eight or nine of them do so. They take that lump sum from the company, use a tax-free rollover into an IRA, and then spend the money from there, in a way that works best for their individual needs. Bottom line positive: you have much more control over your pension money. Let's explore this further.   We recommend that everyone we work with do a retirement income analysis, which provides you with the context you need to make informed decisions about your money.

We develop a retirement income analysis with just about every prospective client that comes into our office, because it is so helpful for individual decision making. A thorough retirement income analysis gives you a benchmark of the amount of money you can take from your investments on a monthly basis given a certain rate of return. It can even show the impact of stock market volatility on your accounts.

For example, let's say that in doing this analysis, you determine that in your retirement - to meet all your goals, in addition to what you will be receiving from Social Security and any other income that you may have - you will need $3,000 a month from your retirement lump sum that has been rolled over into an IRA. The next step is simple - you can start taking $3,000 a month out of that account.

To continue with this scenario, a few months later you decide that you would like to lower that monthly amount to $2,700. Again, quite simple. You just go ahead and lower the amount you receive to $2,700 a month. In fact, I have a client that I've been working with for a few years, and she has changed her monthly payment three or four times.

The changes have not been very large - going from $2,700 to $2,900, up to $3,000 and then back to $2,200. As her needs changed, the payment was easy to adjust. She has appreciated the flexibility to not take out more than she needs, adjusting as her needs changed. As was stated previously, a key advantage of the lump sum is control over the payments, and flexibility. When you change your monthly withdrawals, you can simply have us re-do the retirement income analysis so that you know you're not taking too much out of the account. One more example. Let's say you decide to take a vacation and you want an extra $5,000 or $10,000 out of the account. Maybe you're planning a nice vacation for a special occasion, so it is a $20,000 vacation. You can withdraw $20,000 from that IRA account that you had rolled your pension into without changing the payment amounts. This is another example of control and flexibility – which you would not have if you take the monthly payments from the company and not the lump sum. Yet another advantage of the lump sum is that you can leave it behind. If you (and your spouse if you're married) die before you've exhausted all the money, that money passes on to somebody else.

This is rarely true with a traditional monthly pension. Thus, you would have the ability to leave a legacy to either individuals or charities that you care about, for example, by having control over that lump sum.

One additional potential advantage of the lump sum option is the possibility that you can do considerably better in a good investment environment - if you pick the right investments - than had the money been invested by the company that holds the pension plan. There is the possibility that you could even grow the lump sum while you are taking out the $3,000 each month. In the right investment environment, and with good investment decisions, that lump sum might even double over time. As these examples illustrate, there are many advantages to taking the lump sum, beginning with the "big two" that I focus on - flexibility and control. You have much more flexibility and much more control. That does come, however, with a price - you bear the investment risk, and if you are "bad" with money, for the reasons I've outlined, perhaps it is best that you not have control over that lump sum of money.

Option Two: Monthly Pension Payouts

Now, let's walk through the second basic option, which is that you leave things as they are and the company is on the hook and obligated to pay you a monthly check as long as you live. Here too, there are advantages and disadvantages.

First, let's explore the disadvantages. The primary disadvantage is basically the exact opposite of the advantages to taking the lump sum and rolling it over. With this option, you completely lack flexibility. You can't change the payments, up or down, at all.

You also limit your potential to do better on the investment side. Your payments are locked in, or guaranteed. Although they might have a cost of living allowance, they are otherwise locked in and guaranteed, so you lose the opportunity to do better from an investment standpoint. Most would consider that to be a negative. Some pension plans may also require that you wait until age 65 to begin taking the money – and you usually cannot leave the money behind, in most cases, for somebody outside of your marriage.

Therefore, any remaining funds when you die cannot become legacy money that passes on for 30 or 40 years into the future for children or grandchildren, as it could with an Individual Retirement Account as we discussed earlier. This is going to be money that will likely die with you, or with you and your spouse. When you and your spouse are no longer here, these payments come to an end. There are, however, some positives in choosing to take a monthly payout.

First, you are guaranteed to get those checks as long as you live or as long as you and your spouse live. They will keep coming, month after month, very predictably.

Second, you are effectively forced to be on a budget, because there will not be investment income fluctuations, up or down. So again, as was mentioned earlier, if you are not the best with money or you are concerned that you may pass away first and you are uncertain about what would happen if your spouse inherits the money, you may be better off keeping it in a monthly payment that is guaranteed for the rest of your lives.

There is also an additional negative possibility to consider — if the company goes into bankruptcy. Should the company that is paying your pension fall into bankruptcy, there is a federal agency, the Pension Benefit Guaranty Corporation (PBGC), which, in effect, has your back. (More on that in the next chapter, How Safe Is My Pension?)

Individualized Decision

To provide a real-life example of a couple who considered this choice, lump sum versus monthly payouts, it is worthwhile to walk through our work with a client - a husband and wife we'll call Bob and Betty - who considered with us the choices they had, and what would be the best strategy in their particular circumstances. I have included a chart that highlights Bob and Betty's options — choices that Bob was faced with when he retired from an engineering firm where he had worked for 30 years. As you see on the chart entitled "Pension Estimates," one option that he had was to take a lump sum at age 62, which was the year that he was planning to retire, of $484,276 — indicated as the voluntary lump sum option on the chart.

Slightly farther down are the different options he could take as a pension. You can see that he could take a life annuity of $3,104 per month. If you look just over to the right of that, you will notice that his surviving beneficiary, Betty, would get zero if he died first. If you look further down that column, where you can see his pension choices, you will notice that he could also take what is described as 67 percent joint and survivor with an increase, which means that he could start out receiving $2,678 a month; and if he died, his wife would receive $1,785 per month for the rest of her life. He was leaning towards this option until we examined what could be done if he took the lump sum of $484,276 and rolled it over into an IRA.

Pension Estimates		
Stop Working	62 years 0 months	6/30/2012
Benefit Commencement	62 years 0 months	7/1/2012
Beneficiary	Spouse	
Beneficiary Date of Birth	7/25/1952	
Salary Increase per year	0.0%	
Bonus Amount Paid per year	$15,000.00	
Available Options	**Scenario 1**	
	You	**Spouse**
Cash Balance Plan		
Voluntary Lump Sum	$484,276.80 Lump Sum	N/A
Life Annuity	$3,104.56 Monthly	N/A
100% Joint and Survivor Annuity with Increase	$2,526.93 Monthly	$2,526.93 Monthly
50% Joint and Survivor Annuity with Increase	$2,761.59 Monthly	$1,380.80 Monthly
67% Joint & Survivor with Increase	$2,678.67 Monthly	$1,785.87 Monthly
75% Joint and Survivor with Increase	$2,639.05 Monthly	$1,979.29 Monthly
5 Year Certain and Continuous	$3,044.30 Monthly	$3,044.30 Monthly
10 Year Certain and Continuous	$2,898.44 Monthly	$2,898.44 Monthly
15 Year Certain and Continuous	$2,722.84 Monthly	$2,722.84 Monthly
20 Year Certain and Continuous	$2,553.85 Monthly	$2,553.85 Monthly

There were other considerations that were factored into the analysis specific to this couple – the fact, for example, that Betty was a school teacher who would receive a pension, but a reduced Social Security benefit. That underscores that every circumstance is unique, and the retirement income analysis differs for every individual.

What we were able to do with Bob and Betty, when all was said and done, is to have them take control, as we have discussed, by his electing to take the lump sum instead of taking the monthly payout. Even though the monthly payout was somewhat attractive, Bob determined that he did not really need all the income on a monthly basis that they were offering from the pension, and he preferred to have control over the lump sum. Secondly, he now has all the flexibility. He has his 401(k) and the pension plan; it has all been rolled over into one pot, his IRA. It has been allocated under a wonderful investment program, in which he has a portion of the money in safe indexed annuities that have guaranteed income in the future without stock market risk, and he is taking some income from that.

Additionally, he has a portion of the money in what we call "steady income tools," such as real estate trusts and private equity loan programs, and closed-end mutual funds.

Lastly, he has some money exposed in the traditional stock and bond, mutual fund, and exchange-traded fund portfolios that we typically build for clients.

With that blend, we are targeting a rate of return on that 401(k) of six to seven percent net of all expenses. (Of course, there is no guarantee of future results.) It could well be higher, but let's say six to seven percent, which is more than enough to generate what would have been the pension income, and he has control over the entire lump sum.

Your Pension, Your Choice

What it boils down to is that there is no overarching answer, no one-size-fits-all decision when the choice is to take a lump sum or monthly payouts of your pension benefit. We have laid out for you in this chapter the positives and negatives for each choice. It's up to you and your financial advisor to balance the pros and cons and make the decision that is most suitable for you.

In most instances, the positives outweigh the potential negatives in selecting to take the lump sum. Most people that come into our financial planning practice, after analysis, review and discussing the alternatives, decide to take that lump sum.

But this is a choice that should be made based on your own unique circumstances and situation. Just because most clients take the lump sum and roll it over into an IRA, that does not mean it will be the right thing for you to do. Individual circumstances matter – in fact, they are what matters most. We suggest that you get individualized advice from a member of our firm or some other qualified person that you trust and feel comfortable with, so that you can decide what's best for you and your family.

Chapter 3

How Safe Is My Pension?

This chapter answers an essential question that is asked by individuals on the verge of deciding not to take the lump sum payment from their employer, preferring to depend on the company fulfilling its promise to provide monthly payments for as long as the retired employee lives. The question: If that's what I decide to do, how safe is my pension?

Answering this question is very important to assure that you have peace of mind - knowing how safe your pension will be if you choose not to take the lump sum. We often see articles in the paper or politicians using the phrase "a pension is underfunded" or "the pension hasn't been funded properly." That can lead people to fear that their payments could be in jeopardy.

Having just read that pension payouts are nothing more than a promise to pay, you may have some uncertainty as well.

"What if my company goes broke?" people wonder. "What about United Airlines?" It's been in and out of bankruptcy numerous times. What about General Motors when they went into bankruptcy? What happened to those pensions?

What you need to know is that your pension is guaranteed, with certain limited exceptions, by the federal government. The entity that the federal government has set up is called the Pension Benefit Guaranty Corporation, or PBGC, which you can think of as another guarantee association, much like the FDIC, which you are probably more familiar with - and quite comfortable with. You've probably noticed the FDIC logo on the front of every bank; you're likely less familiar with the PBGC. They work essentially the same way. Companies that have pensions pay a premium into the federal government which in turn ensures that the pension benefits will be paid in the event that the company goes bankrupt.

What type of pension plans does the Pension Benefit Guaranty Corporation stand behind? The answer is, almost all defined benefit plans offered by private sector employers.

Defined benefit plans promise to pay you a specific benefit, usually a monthly amount, beginning at retirement and continuing for the rest of your life.

To illustrate, I have provided a pension benefit guarantee maximum benefit table. It shows, for instance, that a 65-year-old is guaranteed, on a single life basis, up to $5,369.32 per month. As long as your pension isn't over $5,369.32 per month, it's 100 percent guaranteed by the federal government. If you select joint life, then your guaranteed amount is $4,832.39.

PBGC Maximum Monthly Guarantees for 2017		
Age	2017 Straight-Life Annuity	2017 Joint and 50% Survivor Annuity*
75	$16,322.73	$14,690.46
74	$14,840.80	$13,356.72
73	$13,358.87	$12,022.98
72	$11,876.94	$10,689.25
71	$10,395.00	$9,355.50
70	$8,913.07	$8,021.76
69	$8,000.29	$7,200.26
68	$7,194.89	$6,475.40
67	$6,496.88	$5,847.19
66	$5,906.25	$5,315.63
65	$5,369.32	$4,832.39
64	$4,993.47	$4,494.12
63	$4,617.62	$4,155.86
62	$4,241.76	$3,817.58
61	$3,865.91	$3,479.32
60	$3,490.06	$3,141.05
59	$3,275.29	$2,947.76
58	$3,060.51	$2,754.46
57	$2,845.74	$2,561.17
56	$2,630.97	$2,367.87
55	$2,416.19	$2,174.57
54	$2,308.81	$2,077.93
53	$2,201.42	$1,981.28
52	$2,094.03	$1,884.63
51	$1,986.65	$1,787.99
50	$1,879.26	$1,691.33
49	$1,771.88	$1,594.69
48	$1,664.49	$1,498.04
47	$1,557.10	$1,401.39
46	$1,449.72	$1,304.75
45	$1,342.33	$1,208.10

It is important to note that PBGC does not insure three categories of private sector defined benefit plans:

- One is professional service employers with 25 or fewer employees. These are typically doctor's practices, law practices, dentist practices, professional service employers or employers that are classified by professional service. It does not guarantee those pensions. Interestingly enough, most of those professional service employers do not have defined benefit pensions.

- The next category is church groups. PBGC does not insure church groups unless the church group has chosen to be covered. Why? Because when the federal law was passed that said if you have a defined benefit pension it must be guaranteed, that federal law did not apply to church groups because these organizations are exempt from many federal regulations under the Constitution. They can choose to "opt in" and pay the PBGC Insurance premium, and some of the larger church denominations have.

- The third category that the PBGC does not insure are defined benefit pension plans sponsored by federal, state, or local governments. Detroit comes to mind. The Detroit pensions for the people that work for the City of Detroit were not insured by PBGC. That's why it was such a serious matter when Detroit declared bankruptcy and the municipal workers that were promised pensions - and may have already begun to collect pensions - had huge cuts to their benefits because there was no insurance.

As an important reminder, in this discussion we are only talking about defined benefit pension plans and cash balance pension plans. We are not talking about 401(k)'s or 403(b)'s. One of the easiest ways to find out if you are covered by PBGC is to ask your employer or plan administrator for a copy of the summary plan description. I can state with confidence that most private employers – certainly employers in the Northeast - whether it is a big computer company or a defense contractor or a manufacturing company or an insurance company - will have PBGC insurance.

To be absolutely certain, it would be worthwhile to check. Some of the insured plans, including the cash balance plan, may state a promised benefit as a single account balance. This is also covered by the PBGC, but in this chapter we are discussing pensions that pay you a monthly amount.

This chapter has hopefully alleviated concern about the general safety of pension payments if you opt not to take a lump sum. Because of the Pension Benefit Guaranty Corporation, there are sound protections for most pensions, and clear employment situations where PBGC protections do not apply.

If you are to be concerned at all about pension payouts, that concern would be well-placed in regards to state, federal, and city or municipal pensions, and the other exception categories I've mentioned, which are not guaranteed. Paying attention to the safety of those pension plans makes sense – and the absence of a PBGC guarantee may be sufficient motivation to roll that money over, if you are presented with that option, into an Individual Retirement Account.

Chapter 4

What Do I Do First?

You have one major decision to make, but what do you consider first? What factors should you think about, and in what order, so that you can make the best decision?

Here is my suggestion on an effective way to proceed. There are four basic steps and questions that will help you through the decision-making process as you evaluate whether to take a lump sum and roll it over into an Individual Retirement Account, (which means you don't have to take any money at all right away unless you're over 70 ½ years old), or begin taking the monthly payout from your company.

1. Do I need the money at all?

Step number one is really a fundamental question: do you need the money at all? It is a great question to start with because if you do not need this money, if you believe that you are financially okay for retirement, then it presents a wonderful opportunity to pass money on to your children. If that is the case, then you should roll the money over. On the other hand, if you absolutely need the money - and need the monthly payouts - then that will sway your decision in the opposite direction, towards proceeding with the monthly payments. So, the first question you need to ask and answer is, do you need the money at all?

2. Am I responsible with money?

The second question that you should ask yourself - and answer honestly – is, am I responsible with money? We touched on this briefly earlier in this book. This is a critical question, so much so that if you have any hesitation that you can answer this honestly, you may want to ask a close friend for their opinion, and factor their point of view into your consideration.

You need to make sure you're responsible with money and disciplined in following through on your financial plan, long-term. Here's why. Let's say you roll the money over, after a financial advisor has created a detailed long-term plan for you, in which you have decided that a good withdrawal rate on that money is four percent, for example. So, you are taking out enough money each month, consistent with the plan you decided upon based on your needs, totaling approximately four percent per year. Then, all of a sudden, you start going haywire for whatever reason - buying Ferraris and boats, expensive items of that nature, or bailing out your kids with enormous sums, and so on.

That is not being responsible with the money and the very real danger is that you may deplete that money. Money that was supposed to last a lifetime could quickly evaporate. That is why the second question is, am I responsible with money?

3. Can I trust someone to invest my money?

Next, you should ask yourself, can I trust someone to invest my money to generate an income and preserve principal?

For most people, that will mean identifying a financial advisor to work with. That may not be true for everybody, but most people are much better off working with a financial advisor than attempting to navigate the ups and downs of the investment process themselves.

As an investor, your biggest obstacle to investment success is your behavior in times of stress or when things are going really well. When things are going well, people tend to be concerned that they might be missing out on a financial opportunity, so they decide to put more money at risk. When things are going poorly, they panic and they sell out of the market.

It is very easy to say, in a calm moment while reading this book, "Well, I know the market will always come back. I won't do that." I'm here to tell you, based on my experience, that most people do just that. It is human nature, and they just can't help themselves. Thus, most people are better off working with a financial advisor. If you accept the premise that most people are better off working with a financial advisor, and you believe that applies to you, then you need to identify someone you can trust.

You may not be able to know with 100 percent certainty that the financial advisor you select will be a good fit for you and your needs, but you can thoroughly check their credentials, get a sense of the work they've done and the clients they've worked with, and use your own judgement to decide if this is an individual that you can trust. Then you can make a selection with confidence. You can ask, for example, if the retirees they are working with are indeed taking income off of their portfolio, while the principal is preserved. You can ask financial advisors that you are considering to explain what they do and how they do it.

There are certain financial products, for example, which can guarantee a level of payout, in effect mimicking a pension. In fact, you can do a lump sum rollover from your defined benefit pension into an IRA and then turn around and take some of the money in that IRA and buy what looks like a guaranteed pension, from an insurance company.
That is just one of the many possible approaches. That's why the key is whether you can work with someone you trust to invest your money to generate income and preserve principal.

4. How will this decision affect those I love?

The final of the four central questions you need to answer is, when I die, how will this decision affect those I love?

When you pass on, is it going to hurt your children that because you took a monthly payout - and now all of a sudden that has ended - you are unable to leave them anything? Especially if you had wanted to leave something to the kids and grandkids? Perhaps that outcome is not acceptable to you.

On the other hand, what if you opt to take the lump sum, but then you do not invest it wisely, or you take too much income out of it, and the result is that you run out of money? Is that going to affect your loved ones, because they must now have to bail out Mom and Dad? Well, that could be a problem, too. That is why it is important to consider, how will this decision affect those I love?

Those are the four central questions that you should be able to answer to help you make the choice as to whether to take a lump sum or monthly payments in retirement. For some of those questions, it can be tremendously helpful to get outside input from a financial professional who customarily works with retirees - someone you feel comfortable with, and who will provide you with truthful answers and honest input. That can make all the difference in the world, as you decide which option is best for you.

To briefly review, here are the four questions that you ought to answer before you move forward with a decision on whether to take a lump sum or monthly payments in retirement:

1. Do I need this money at all?

2. Am I responsible with money?

3. Can I trust someone to invest my money and generate an income and preserve principal?

4. When I die, how will this decision affect those I love?

As you consider what to do first in working through whether to choose to take the lump sum retirement payment your company is offering, or the monthly payments for life, the answers to these questions will help guide your decision.

Chapter 5

Do I Need a Retirement Income Analysis?

In this chapter, we will spend some time discussing the importance of having a solid retirement income analysis and income projection prepared for you to carefully consider. Having that done is, in my view, essential to sound decision-making.

As part of our Money Map Retirement Review at Johnson Brunetti, we call this Retirement Analyzer, but there are many programs available online that may provide similar information for you. I suggest that you have an analysis done with a financial advisor who has specific expertise in the retirement planning area, and especially a professional with clients that are already retired. I suggest this because they are much more likely to know about real-life circumstances that an online program just can't spit out or doesn't know to ask you.

Having a retirement income analysis done, which is a process that a good financial advisor can take you through, will let you know two essential elements of a sound decision.

First, it will let you know, based on your goals and how much income you want - factoring in all the other elements of your income, such as social security, brokerage accounts and so on - if you have enough money to last for the rest of your life.

Here's basically how it works. You tell the financial advisor how much monthly income you want, after taxes. Let's say that it is $15,000 a month, after taxes. They run the numbers, factor in inflation and other variables and tell you whether you are likely to be okay financially through age 95 or 100. You can see how important it is to know, as you make this decision, whether you will still have money available to you from your retirement at age 95 or 100. That would certainly indicate that you're in a good financial position.

Second, it will help you to determine the rate of return you will need over the long-term. One of the assumptions that goes into this retirement income analysis is a certain rate of return that is assumed on your investment accounts. So one approach is to, in effect, figure this out backwards.

Here's what I mean. You could say, let me find out what rate of return I need on my investment accounts to be okay for the rest of my life, to meet all my retirement income goals. Then one of the ways we use retirement income analysis is by running the numbers with different rates of return figured in, to find out what rate of return you would need for your money to last to age 95 or 100.

On the next page is an example of one page of our retirement income analysis. It shows that, in this case, our client runs out of money at age 97. Everyone's situation is different. I could be working with one couple that needs only a 4 percent rate of return to meet all their goals. I could have another couple that needs an 8 percent rate of return. Of course, an 8 percent rate over the long term when you're taking money off a portfolio is somewhat aggressive. So, we would have to be careful that we're not being too aggressive with our withdrawals and analyze further the level of need that the couple believes they have.

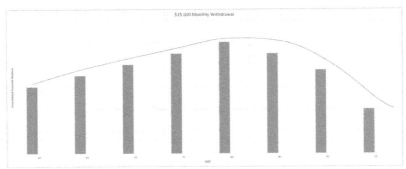

Doing a thorough analysis allows you to have those discussions now, before you make your decision, rather than later, when it would be much more difficult, with potentially adverse financial consequences.

That is why I firmly believe that a retirement income analysis is so important – it tells you two critical things: number one, are you going to be financially okay, and number two, what rate of return do you need to be okay. The results of that analysis can help you to arrive at an answer that is right for you and your particular circumstances, needs and objectives.

Chapter 6

What are the Risks and Rewards?

It is important to look at the risks and rewards of your potential choices when you consider whether or not to take a lump sum upon retirement. As discussed earlier, this may be one of the most important decisions that you make – with financial and quality of life consequences that, quite literally, last a lifetime.

Most of the people that we have counseled over the years at my firm - between myself and the other financial advisors - take the lump sum option, as I explained in a previous chapter. They roll their pension over into an IRA, where they have more flexibility and control.

It is important, however, to take as balanced approach as possible in discussing this choice, because it is very important that you understand the pure risks and the pure rewards of each of your choices. You want to look at the ramifications, including considering the worst-case scenario

- so that you can make the right decision for you and your family. So, let's go through some of the risks and the rewards.

To wrap up this chapter, I will share with you an easy-to-understand chart which will enable you to simply take a highlighter and highlight those approaches that you care about most. That will help you see – quite literally – what the best decision would be, reflecting your own individual preferences, concerns and objectives.

Taking the Lump Sum

If you elect to take the lump sum rollover, here are the risks and rewards. At the top of the list of rewards is that you get total control of your money. You can withdraw it as you want when you want or leave it invested and untouched. You can leave it behind for heirs. You can leave what's remaining to charity, if you haven't used all the funds through your retirement years. First and foremost, you get total control of your money.

The second reward of taking the lump sum is that you get investment flexibility. That offers a range of options – and provides you the ability to buy just about any of the many investment vehicles you are probably familiar with in the marketplace, such as CDs, stocks, bonds, annuities and various types of commodity funds. You could buy institutional portfolios of real estate as well. The choice becomes yours.

If you establish a self-directed IRA, for example, you could choose to buy individual real estate or private partnerships, although we do not recommend that. In most instances, you would rollover the lump sum into your investment account, a traditional IRA and diversify the funds among more traditional investments.

As was mentioned previously, you also have the ability to pass this money – or a portion of it - on to who you choose, whether it may be children or grandchildren, or charities. Another plus in taking the lump sum is that it enables you to change the amount you receive at will, even every month if you choose to, or take special withdrawals to meet occasional retirement needs that may arise. For example, you can take out money in order to make gifts, or for other purposes or occasions. The bottom line is that the top-of-the-list reward for taking the lump sum is that you will have total control over how you invest the money and how you choose to withdraw the money.

There are also some downsides to taking the lump sum and rolling over your pension into an IRA. If you are not yet age 59 ½, - this is an important point - if you take money out of that IRA that you've rolled your money into, you may be required to pay a ten percent penalty on withdrawals. This is not a ten percent penalty on the entire amount in your IRA, it is only a ten percent penalty on the withdrawal.

Here is an example: Let's say that you take $1 million from a pension fund, roll it over into an IRA, and you are 57 years old. If you withdraw $100,000, you are going to have to add that $100,000 to your tax return as income, just as you would if you had taken pension payments. But because you are not 59 ½, you will have to pay an additional ten percent on that $100,000. As is quite evident, this is a negative, and explains why individuals will sometimes set up a different account to access before they reach age 59½.

Another risk in taking the lump sum is that you lose that income guarantee – the check that arrives every month, like clockwork. This can be offset if you were to take some of the money and buy a pension style annuity, which would provide the predictable monthly income on that piece of your retirement lump sum. That is why many people - and let's use that million-dollar example again - might rollover the entire $1 million into an IRA, and then take a half-million dollars, 50 percent of that, and put it into an annuity where they would receive an income guarantee. They can rely on that income, month after month, for the rest of their lives, and they also have control over the $500,000. Some people view this as the best of both worlds, financially speaking.

Those are some of the risks and rewards of one of the options you need to consider when choosing the lump sum rollover. Now let's talk about the risks and rewards of electing to take the monthly pension payout amount.

Taking the Monthly Payout

On the reward side, you get lifetime payments guaranteed by the company. As we stated earlier, you could do that with an annuity, but you can also get the guaranteed lifetime payments from the actual pension fund. It protects against poor spending decisions in years to come, and can serve to protect you and your retirement funds from dependents or others who may come to you looking for money or from your own habitually poor spending habits. This approach could also provide a potentially higher payout rate than trying to replicate this on your own with an insurance company. It is important to consult a financial advisor who has expertise in annuities to compare an annuity payout from an insurance company to the payout guaranteed by the company.

Let's take a moment to compare the payout rate from your pension against the lump sum that we outlined earlier in this chapter. Let's say, again, that you have a $1 million lump sum, versus a payout rate of $6,000 a month. The payout of $6,000 a month equals $72,000 a year. Therefore, the cash flow payout rate on that $1 million is 7.2 percent. That may be a higher payout rate than you can get elsewhere. That is why you should compare the rate to what you might be able to get if you invest the money.

Although by taking the monthly pension payout you have given up control of the money, the positive, or reward, is that you remove your downside risk. The negative, or downside, of taking that monthly payment amount is your loss of flexibility. You no longer have control over the assets. You cannot pass the money on, and you limit your investment upside. Let's go through each of those risks and rewards.

First, the loss of flexibility. I believe we've walked through this sufficiently, and at this point it is clear to you. If you take a monthly payout, you don't have any flexibility in the payments, nor do you have upside or downside with the investments. You no longer have an asset you can pass on, because there is not an asset. Rather, there is a stream of payments, technically with a value, but basically a stream of payments guaranteed for you and your spouse's life.

Second, because you don't have an asset that you are able to reach, you limit your investment upside. You are merely going to receive monthly payments.

If you roll that money over and invest it at a higher rate than the payout amount, you could ultimately amass a much larger amount of money. For example, you might earn eight or nine percent, or more, on your money, compared with taking the payout, where you are going to receive only the monthly payout, which is a combination of principal and interest.

I have developed a quick-and-easy chart that lists the rewards and risks of the monthly pension payout and the lump sum rollover, so you can evaluate the options for yourself and determine what's best for you. I would suggest highlighting (with a highlighter marker!) the aspects of each choice that matter most to you. I would also recommend that you make this decision with the counsel of an experienced CERTIFIED FINANCIAL PLANNER™ rather than attempting to do this on your own.

A professional with training and expertise in the field may be aware of some aspects of the decision, including specific challenges that other people have encountered, that you may not be familiar with or even aware of. While I am appreciative that you are reading this book, reading may not be enough to make the best decision for your individual financial circumstances and goals. There are a great many intangibles to consider, including the human element of this incredibly important pension decision.

	RISK	REWARD
Lump Sum	You bear the investment risk.	You have control and flexibility in investing , accessing and receiving your retirement money.
	You give up guaranteed monthly payment.	
	If you have not reached age 59½ there would be a withdrawal penalty.	You can pass money on to children, grandchildren or charities.
Monthly Payments	You lose all your financial flexibility.	Guaranteed lifetime payments.
	You don't have an asset to pass on, to descendants or charity.	Protection against poor spending decisions or people asking for money.

Chapter 7

What Are The 6 Things Not To Do?

I imagine that by this point you are getting a good sense of how important this decision is - and that it does not need to be an overly complicated decision. It really should not be completely overwhelming or the source of apprehension.

The goal here is to provide you with enough information to enable you to confidently make the decision that's right for you and your family. As much as that means suggesting what you ought to do, it also means alerting you to what not to do.

There are six things that could quite possibly ruin your future, and I mean that in all seriousness. As I proceed to outline them, I may have a little fun in the presentation, but the concerns are very real. These admonitions all are based in real experiences – people have made these mistakes and they have actually done what is described below.

Here we go:

1. *Don't Try to Outsmart the System*

As you move through your pension decision, do not check with all of your fellow engineers or people who have a deep admiration for Excel spreadsheets. It is not a good idea to sit with them to compare spreadsheets on the various pension payout options, their variances, create some kind of a delta, and figure out a way to game the pension or get what you believe will be the hands-down guaranteed way to get the most money out of the system. First of all, you are quite likely wasting your time. Second, due to the way you are thinking about the problem – and I say engineers in fun here, but engineers tend to be guilty of this – you miss the big picture in many cases.

If you look at the payout options from a mathematical standpoint, because life expectancy is involved, (for you, and if you are putting your spouse on the pension, for both of you), they are all equal from an actuarial standpoint. You are just not going to create a spreadsheet that makes you smarter than almost every insurance company in the

United States. Really? It's not going to happen. The only way to beat the system is by living a longer life than they anticipate. That's it.

Of course, they have the law of large numbers on their side. You are making an isolated decision, and by its very nature an isolated decision increases your risk versus when there are a lot of people in the pool. It is not at all beneficial or helpful to create a complex spreadsheet and attempt to figure out what the best option may be. The best option is the option that's best for you and your family. You are not going to figure out or uncover a hidden mathematical anomaly that some $15 to $25 billion pension fund has missed, try as you might.

Now, we're having a little fun here, but those of you who are actuaries and engineers, you may indeed believe that you can outsmart the system. Based on my experience, I'm here to tell you that you will not. And I wouldn't want you to embarrass yourself by trying – or make a financial decision that does more harm than good.

Along the same lines, I would also stay away from analyzing the options in the belief that you are going to discover some way to get more money one way or the other that no one has managed to figure out before. Even if you are smarter than most people, you shouldn't expect to figure out a methodology that a huge publicly traded company with the help of outside consultants has somehow missed. Again, it's not going to happen.

2. Don't Turn This into a Public Opinion Poll

Asking around is a sure way to make a poor decision. Turning to co-workers, neighbors, or club members to ask about the pension decision they are going to make, in the belief that if most people are doing something it is probably the right thing to do, is a mistake. The reality is that if most people are doing something in the world of investments, it is just as likely that it is the wrong thing to do. Human nature, however, often leads us to conclude it is safer if we do what most people are doing. Not true. In the investment world, doing what most people are doing is almost a sure way to go broke!

This decision is yours to make, based on your own particular circumstances - it is not a public opinion poll. It must be the right choice for you and your family. Your family is different and distinct from the people you are talking with, no matter how similar they may seem. As a professional in this business for many years, I have seen people blindsided over and over again because they make what they believe is the safe choice only because it is the most popular opinion. More often than not, in today's world, most people are doing the wrong thing. Here's another reason not to follow the crowd. Innovation, by its very nature, is proof that the crowd is usually wrong. If you consider Warren Buffett to be a good investor, or that innovations like the iPhone and Google and Facebook or the discoveries made by drug companies that help keep us alive longer and heal diseases, are real, then clearly the crowd was wrong.

So, don't take a public opinion poll. This is a decision that needs to be made solely on what you are looking to achieve for you and your family.

3. Speaking of Google... Don't Rely on What Google Tells You

As wonderful as Google is, typing in the words "pension buyout versus pension payments" is not the way to decide what to do. To begin with, you will instantly be bombarded by *advertising* from some of the large brokerage firms and insurance firms and your computer will start to smoke and catch fire.

Well no, probably not that, but there are going to be an endless array of opinions, options and variations as you scroll down through site after site opining on whether to take a pension payout or the monthly pension buyout. You will be hit with what appears to be valid advice from so-called experts that, truth be told, are often little more than either Ivy League hipsters that have considerably less money than you, or financial planners trying to sell you a product. So please be careful. Remember, the Internet doesn't have much of a filter. You might unknowingly be receiving financial advice from someone still in school who lives in their parents' basement - and their parents are still paying their car insurance, cell phone bill, and health insurance premiums. You may be seeing their advice because they have an internet following – which means absolutely nothing in terms of the validity of their advice. This is a very important individual financial decision. You need to receive individualized advice, not generic advice from an Internet site.

4. Don't Think They're Out to Get You

Individuals can also get in financial trouble, making bad decisions, if you wrongly conclude that the company paying out the pension is trying to rip you off. For whatever reason, some people have the impression that most large companies are trying to figure out a way to rip them off, so they decide to insist on some kind of a full accounting - or something totally unreasonable and not based in fact. I assure you, in my career, I have never seen a company that is trying to rip off the employee. Rather, when it comes to pension payments, most if not all are doing their best to fulfill the promises that they've made to their employees. I would add that it is this type of thinking that is completely counterproductive as well as incorrect, and I would discourage you from holding the misimpression that the company is trying to rip you off and you just need to figure out how. You will use much time and energy unproductively, and your unwarranted fear will inhibit your ability to make a good decision on how to take your retirement funds, Plus, if this is your approach to life you will probably forever be cynical and miserable to be around!

5. Don't Freak Out or Tighten Up

Yes, it is an important financial decision which can have an impact on the rest of your life, but you do not want to freak out. Don't get so nervous and so uptight about this decision that your ability to make the best decision for you and your family becomes impossible. Having perspective can help. For most people, the decision at hand is only one part of an overall retirement plan. There may be some individuals who have not saved any money and will rely solely on their pension and social security. But for most people reading this book, there is a more comprehensive financial portfolio, which may include brokerage accounts, 401(k)s, other savings, and you will also begin to receive Social Security payments. This pension decision is, therefore, but one part of an overall retirement plan - so you should not freak out or get overwhelmed by this decision. Consult a financial planner and make sure that whatever path you take, whether it is the pension payout, the monthly pension payout, or the rollover into an IRA to invest the money, you consider, with a financial advisor, the worst case scenario - and make sure you can recover from the worst case scenario. Planning may be the best preventative to tightening up, or freaking out.

6. Don't Let a Relative Decide For You

There is one additional "don't" on the list - don't ask your son, brother, cousin, niece, or relative of a close friend to tell you what you should do. I have seen individuals who have the attitude "Well, my son works at the bank, so he must know what to do" or "My daughter went to Brown University" or "he graduated from Yale and majored in finance. He certainly must know what to do." You cannot begin to imagine the damage I've seen done when parents decide that their son or daughter who works at the local bank knows everything there is to know about money. That is not necessarily a conclusion that you want to reach – or one that will help you.

First of all, your son or daughter or cousin or nephew will probably not have any idea what you're going through and the factors that should enter into your decision. Simply put, they're not you. So make sure you receive customized advice and be careful about getting advice from people who, although they may have your best interest at heart, don't know what they don't know. I am aware of numerous examples of people who would come into our office, listen to our recommendation, and then would call their young adult child who works at XYZ bank. I shudder to think how many times I've heard the son or daughter respond along the lines of "Well, you better not do that because I read on an internet financial site that you should do XYZ" or "I read in a financial magazine that you should do XYZ" - and so the parent listens to the advice and does XYZ, only to return to us two or three years later after all kinds of damage has been done to their future retirement and their investment portfolio. Again, if you are tempted to let a relative decide for you, just say no (thank you).

Chapter 8

Should I Have A Retirement Income and Financial Plan?

The answer is a resounding yes! Throughout this book, I have mentioned the importance of making your pension decision in the context of the rest of your financial picture. Whether you elect to take a lump sum and roll it over into an IRA and create your own stream of income or you choose to take the monthly payments, it should not be an isolated decision. I strongly encourage everyone reading this book to develop an overall retirement plan or financial plan. It is, in my professional opinion, absolutely essential. Financial planning is defined as "the process of determining whether and how an individual can meet life goals through the proper management of financial resources."

Financial planning integrates the financial planning process with the financial planning subject areas. The basic subject areas typically covered in the financial planning process include:

- Financial statement preparation and analysis (including cash flow analysis/planning and budgeting)
- Insurance planning and risk management
- Employee benefits planning
- Investment planning
- Income tax planning
- Retirement planning
- Estate planning

To develop your financial plan, using the professional services of a CERTIFIED FINANCIAL PLANNER™ is the way to go. What does that mean?

I am one of the many of the people at our firm who are CERTIFIED FINANCIAL PLANNER™ professionals. That means we have taken courses and passed a very rigorous test (the CFP Certification Examination) to become a CERTIFIED FINANCIAL PLANNER™. (About one-third of those who take the test nationally do not pass and just to take the test once must take courses and tests in many different subject areas.)

We also have to continue taking educational courses and demonstrate to the Certified Financial Planning Board that we are up-to-date with our educational requirements. In addition, we must maintain a higher ethical standard and a higher fiduciary standard that have been in place for many, many years through the CFP® Board that, quite frankly, many people in our business do not have to adhere to.

To proceed through the financial planning process, there are six key steps outlined by the CERTIFIED FINANCIAL PLANNER™ Board of Standards. We call it retirement income plan in our firm, because almost all of our clients are either retired or within ten years of retirement. It can, however, be referred to as a retirement plan or a financial plan. Here are the six steps:

1. Establishing and Defining the Client-Planner Relationship

At the outset, we want to have a conversation. This could be in writing, but does not necessarily need to be. What is important is to make certain that you understand the client-planner relationship. What is your relationship as a client with the financial planner or the retirement planner?

What will it look like? How often will you meet? What is the fee structure? What are the expectations? You may also want to find out what type of clients the advisor specializes in working with. At the start, first on the list, is to establish, define and understand the client-planner relationship.

2. Gather Client Data Including Goals

Next, the advisor needs to gather your financial data, including your goals. Gathering data to put your plan together includes two different elements. First, what is called hard data? Where is your money? How much is your Social Security going to be? When do you plan to retire? How is your money invested? Are there any special circumstances or changes coming down the pike that we need to know about? Those are all hard facts.

The other element is goals. That should include your fears and aspirations - what we call the soft facts. They are just as important as the hard facts. So, the second step in establishing a good retirement plan or financial plan is the advisor gathering client data and goals.

3. Analyzing and Evaluating the Client's Current Financial Status

The advisor next needs to analyze and evaluate your current financial status as compared to your goals. Many times what we see when individuals come into our office is that there is a disconnect between what they say is important and how their money is invested. As you might imagine, it is very important that the financial advisor analyzes and evaluates your current financial status and then compares that with your goals.

4. Developing and Presenting Recommendations and/or Alternatives

With data in hand, and objectives understood, the financial advisor develops and presents to you, the client, specific alternatives for you to consider and recommendations on how best to proceed. Those recommendations may or may not endorse your current situation. The recommendation may be to make adjustments to have your planning match your goals more closely. That may require a change in what you are currently doing.

5. Implementing the Recommendations

If you choose to have the financial planner proceed to implement the recommendations that have been presented to you, then that becomes the next step. This would occur after a discussion in which you are presented with recommendations in detail, so that you understand and are comfortable with the recommendations, and agree that they are consistent with your financial goals. If the recommendations are provided to you, but never implemented by the financial planner on your behalf, you are at risk of never following through on the recommendations. This unfortunately is many times the case when a client is left to follow through on recommendations on their own.

The only time you would want the financial planner not to follow through is if you are uncomfortable with, or you don't trust, the financial advisor. If you trust the financial advisor and believe that their actions are in your best interest, and they have presented a plan that makes sense to you based on your goals, then they should continue.

Under those circumstances, you should allow them to make the changes that have been recommended for your portfolio and go ahead to manage that money.

6. Monitoring the Recommendations

There is one additional step, and it is important. A good financial planner will monitor the recommendations.

For example, in our firm we want to get together for a face-to-face meeting with our clients that have at least once each year. There should also be automated systems in place to manage client portfolios so the firm can effectively serve many clients without someone "falling through the cracks" as a result of human error.

Of course, we talk with many clients several times and see them more often than that during the year, but we believe it is prudent to revisit the plan at least once per year to make sure the recommendations are still in line with what each client's individual goals and objectives. It also provides us with an opportunity to find out from our client if any of their goals have changed during the year. For all of these reasons, this final step is as important as those that preceded it.

Our Process

At Johnson Brunetti, we call our retirement planning process the Money Map Retirement Review, and it follows the steps that we have outlined here, consistent with the CERTIFIED FINANCIAL PLANNER™ Board of Standards. The first thing that we do when somebody comes in to our office is begin to establish a client relationship. Often individuals who come in for an initial visit have learned about our firm either through the local TV program that I do, or they've listened to my radio program, or they've attended a workshop that I have led, so they know just a little bit about us and they're interested in knowing more. Establishing a client relationship is our first step. Next, as we talk about what a relationship with us would look like, we walk you through the Money Map Retirement Review process. In fact, you don't even have to engage us to have us go through that process with you. We then would as you a series of questions and gather your data.

Most importantly, as was explained earlier in this chapter, we would ask about your goals, objectives, fears, and aspirations. Then we analyze your data and we compare it against what you're already doing.

We will analyze your current accounts. We will look at when you're planning to take Social Security, whether that is the right time, and whether you have any pension decisions on the horizon. What about dependents? Are they likely to need any help from you in the future? We will completely analyze your particular situation. Then, based on our expertise, we will develop and outline individualized recommendations for you.

Our analysis consists of two main elements. One is a risk analysis of your portfolio, and we have a process to develop that analysis. The other is a retirement income plan in which we design, specifically for you, a retirement income plan that answers two main questions:

- Are you going to be okay with the money that you've saved and the income sources that you have – will you be able to meet all your goals and will your money last for the rest of your life?

- What financial rate of return do you need on your assets, over time, to meet those goals?

We then match the retirement income plan with the risk analysis to find out if you're on the right track and if it is possible that you will be able to reach the goals that you have.

Then, when we present a recommendation to you, which is the next step, we show you those two elements, the retirement income plan plus the risk analysis, and we discuss them.

Some people prefer to see a hard copy; others prefer to have a conversation. Our approach is to present to you, on one page, a clear and concise description of your current financial picture, then carefully explain what we recommend, and we actually walk you through that in a conversation. That's why we call it the Money Map. It does look like a map.

Then, if you choose to work with us and have us proceed as we have recommended, we will implement those recommendations and monitor on an ongoing basis.

Our process lines up with the CERTIFIED FINANCIAL PLANNER™ Board of Standards and we continue to adhere to those standards by monitoring the relationship over time to make sure that if any changes occur in specific circumstances or goals, we adjust for it. Obviously, you need to inform us when goals change. In that way, we are meeting the highest professional standards and doing our utmost for you, our client.

Conclusion

As these chapters have described, this may be one of the most important decisions that you make – with financial and quality of life consequences that, quite literally, last a lifetime. But it does not need to be overwhelming, debilitating or frightening. When that moment arrives, you will have a decision to make: monthly payments, or lump sum. That is the question. It is your pension, and your choice.

Your pension is a promise that the company made to you when your employment began, to provide you with money when you retire. Because the company has made you that promise, at some time in the future they are going to have to pay out money to you. That's good news. Now, the choices begin. From the company's standpoint, they are likely to offer you a lump sum instead of monthly payments, when you retire.   Your deciding to take the lump sum has definite advantages for the company, but not necessarily for you.

They would really rather not have that future liability sitting there on their balance sheet, and be done with it. But you need to decide what is best for you, and your family.

You have options, and they ought to be considered carefully. If you take a monthly payout, the risk is on the company. You receive a steady, predictable stream of income in retirement. On the other hand, if you decide to take a lump sum payment, you have many potential benefits, but you are now responsible for investing the money. As the saying goes, it's on you.

When you are facing this decision, it is important to understand that your pension is guaranteed, with certain limited exceptions, by the federal government. If you fall into one of those exceptions, that may influence the decision you make. If not, you should have peace of mind about the security of those payments over the long term. As you contemplate how to proceed, carefully evaluating your options is essential to make an informed decision. There are a number of questions worth considering.

Among them: Are you responsible with money? Can you trust someone to invest your money? How will your decision – lump sum or monthly pension payments – affect loved ones?

A Retirement Income Analysis will also provide you with a better understanding of the impact of each of your choices. There are risks and rewards with both options, whether you opt to take the lump sum or the monthly payments. It is worth carefully considering them in the context of your own individual financial objectives and concerns. This is not a cookie-cutter decision - one size does not fit all. Everyone's individual circumstances differ from other family members, or co-workers, or neighbors, or club members. Referencing a simple chart (see page 62) can help you come to a decision on which choice is best for you and your family. As you evaluate what you should do, it is also important to be aware of what you shouldn't do. Don't try to outsmart the system (you won't be able to), definitely do not rely on what you find in an Internet search, don't turn this into a public opinion poll by asking everyone you encounter what to do, and don't let a relative – however well meaning – decide for you. I can't emphasize enough how important it is for you to put this decision in a financial context, specific to your own financial circumstances and objectives. The best way to do that is to have an overall retirement plan, or financial plan.

Regardless of what you call it, having such an analysis done, in accordance with best practices adhered to by a CERTIFIED FINANCIAL PLANNER™, can make a significant difference as you weigh the options with retirement just around the corner, and are faced with the pension decision of your life.

Note from the Author

Thank you for picking up this book, and taking the time to read through it. Hopefully, it has been very helpful for you, as you look ahead to the not-too-distant future when you will be faced with that all-important decision – whether to take monthly payments from your company, or the lump sum that is offered to you at retirement.

I've tried to present the material in a way that will provide you with an effective framework to move through your decision-making process, suggesting ways for you to evaluate your choices, understand your options, and make the best possible decision for you and your family.

As I've mentioned, this is your decision. Every circumstance – financial and otherwise – is different. But there are steps you can take, as I've attempted to lay out clearly and concisely, that can provide the facts you need to make an informed decision.

Knowing the critical questions that need to be asked, being aware of the data and analysis that can inform your decision, and understanding that it's worth the time, effort and energy to proceed along the steps I've outlined can help to give you the confidence you need to make your decision. We have helped a great many clients at Johnson Brunetti respond to this critical financial decision regarding their retirement payment. For many people, it is a choice they have not thought about, or considered at all, during their career and working years. All of a sudden, it seems, they need to decide.

Our firm has extensive experience working with retirees – and soon-to-be retirees – in a wide range of circumstances, and much of the wisdom that we offer comes from understanding what other retirees have gone through as they enter their retirement years. As the saying goes, knowledge is power. And through our experience and professional expertise, we seek to empower you – and work with you, every step of the way. The importance of this decision can't be overestimated. What you decide will have ramifications for your financial security and your quality of life. But you absolutely can make a wise decision – one that is best for you.

Again, thank you for spending time with this book, and the information that has been shared. Please keep in mind the steps that have been outlined here, and don't hesitate to turn to us for help. That's why we're here.